AND THE TERRIBLE STINK

Book Cover and Illustrations by Dakota Hutcheson
Layout and editing by Yevheniia Melnyk

1st edition 2024

ISBN: 979-8-99-050610-7

I would like to tell you about my friend Q. He is creative and kind. He is also very curious and very courageous.

Sometimes, his curiosity and courage get him into trouble.

This is the story of The Terrible Stink.

One day, Q and I were walking to math class.
He wanted to tell me something exciting.

He told me that his mom took him
to a store that sold pranks.

One prank was called "stink bottles," and they can make a room smell really, really bad. Bad like rotten eggs.

When we got to the classroom,
the teacher was not there.

If this ever happens, it is good
to just wait quietly and patiently.

However, Q had something else in mind.
He wanted to try his new stink bottles.

Q started telling other kids in the class about the stink bottles. I felt that he was not really going to try it in our math classroom.

But all of the other students wanted Q to do it. To set off a stink bottle! They were shouting "Do it!" over and over again.

Q paused. I think he knew it was not the right thing to do. But then, one student shouted, "LET IT RIP!" And he did.

As Q got ready to launch the stink bottle, our classmates were yelling "Go Q!", "Yeah!", and "Woo-hoo!" I think this made Q happy.

When the bottle broke on the ground,
our classmates were less happy.

"Eww!"
"Yuck!"
You could hear these words coming from our classroom. It really did smell terrible.

CLASS
HAHAHA!! IT SMELLS TERRIBLE! LIKE ROTTEN EGGS HAHAHA!!
YUCK

I was standing near the door, and I could see other people in the school wondering what that smell was. And our teacher was on her way to the classroom!

UM... Q, I SEE THE TEACHER COMING...

I think she knew that something
was happening in our classroom.
Before she got there, Q decided to leave!

I'M GETTING OUT OF HERE!
THIS WON'T BE GOOD...

Q left the classroom before the teacher came in.

"Who did this?" she asked in a very serious voice. She could see the broken stink bottle on the ground. No one in the class said anything.

WHERE DID Q GO?

"Where did Q go?"
The teacher asked this to the whole class, but she was looking right at me! I was feeling very nervous. I was also worried about my friend Q.

The teacher told all the kids to leave the classroom while she opened a window.

A lot of other people from the school were coming to investigate the terrible stink. Now I was really worried about my friend.

I THINK I WILL TALK TO Q ABOUT COMING FORWARD.

I found Q hiding. He was still laughing.
It still smelled terrible.

I told him our teacher was looking for him.
She was the least happy!

A LOT OF PEOPLE ARE UNHAPPY. AND IT SMELLS REALLY, REALLY BAD.

Q realized that it would be better for him to admit he had done something wrong instead of trying to hide from it.

EVERYONE IN CLASS REALLY WANTED YOU TO DO IT. THAT MUST HAVE BEEN HARD.

Q told the teacher that he was the one who set off the stink bottle. She was disappointed with Q. But she was also disappointed with the whole class.

She told us all about something called "peer pressure."

It means that sometimes kids and grown-ups
do things they do not agree with but only because
of how other people are making them feel.

Q had to help clean up the mess, and the school
smelled terrible for the rest of the day.
And Q learned a valuable lesson.

I WILL TRY NOT TO GIVE INTO PEER PRESSURE!
WE ALL LEARNED TODAY!
Cleane

About the author

Dr. Reshan Richards is a career educator and occasional entrepreneur. Since 2016, he has served as Lecturer at the Columbia University School of Professional Studies in the Human Capital Management program teaching courses on Organizational Strategy and Learning and Leadership Development. For over a decade, he has served as Adjunct Assistant Professor at Teachers College, Columbia University where he teaches courses on Educational Technology, Design Thinking, and Leadership & Technology. He served as CEO of Explain Everything, a whiteboard software company which he co-founded in 2011 until its acquisition in 2022.

He has co-authored several non-fiction books for organizational leaders including *Blending Leadership* published by Wiley-Jossey-Bass in 2016 and *Make Yourself Clear* published by Wiley in 2019. He continues to co-author a monthly subscription newsletter called Making the Case.

He has an Ed.D. in Instructional Technology and Media from Teachers College, Columbia University, an Ed.M in Learning and Teaching from Harvard University, and a B.A. in Music from Columbia University. He lives in Ridgefield, CT with his family and their lovable mutt, Charlie Brown.

Milton Keynes UK
Ingram Content Group UK Ltd.
UKHW050142080624
443643UK00003B/12

9 798990 506107